Mud Pie

For Chet and Heather

Always make
"Mud Pies!"
Judy Morrisett Hopkins

Mud Pie

Written by
Judy Morrisett Hopkins

Illustrated by
Emily Daniels Butler

Chocolate Gravy Books

A Chocolate Gravy Book
Published by Chocolate Gravy Books

Text copyright © 2003
by Judy Morrisett Hopkins

Illustrations copyright © 2005
Emily Daniels Butler

Layout and design
by Judy Morrisett Hopkins

ISBN 1-59872-254-9

1st printing 2005

Judy Morrisett Hopkins, 1946-
Mud Pie
Published by Choclate Gravy Books
1853 Ready Drive,
Hernando, MS 38632

For Chet and Heather,
my wonderful children,

from Mom,
who lived the life of "in a tizzy."

For Brandi and Andi,
my beautiful granddaughters.

Thank you, Robbie,
for your love,
patience, and support.

Thank you, Emily,
for your beautiful work and not giv-
ing up on me.

And, to all my family and friends who
encouraged me, thank you for believ-
ing in me and this book.

And in memory of my precious
mother, Christina White Young

"Lord, make me to know my end, and what is the measure of my days. That I may know how frail I am. Indeed, You have made my days as handbreadths, And my age is nothing before You: Certainly every man at his best state is but 'vapor.'"

Psalms 39:4-5 (NKJV)

"Momma, Momma,
come to see.

*T*he sun is shining

bright on me.

The rain is gone.

The thunder's passed.

We can make

Mud Pies

at last.

I remember what

Grandmother told me about you

as a little girl.

She said

you would make

Mud Pies

and get mud in your golden curls.

*S*he said you took a

Glob

of mud and a

little touch

of sand

and molded it and shaped it

into a little

Chocolate

Man.

*S*he said you would

place him on a

BIG
red stone

to dry.

Then you would name him

and *Sing* to him

Chocolate

Lullabies."

"Oh,

Hannah, Hannah,

I do declare.

It's been so long since I had

golden hair.

It's been so long since I could play.

It's always been

'another day.'

*a*s you can see, gray's

creeping in;

I'm now FAT

where I once was thin.

Deep *wrinkles* now kiss

my skin. Can't you see my

double chin?

I'm so sorry,

*S*weet *H*annah,

I'm just

too, too BUSY.

I'm running late. My life is

in a

TIZZY!

 The computer's

CRASheD.

It has a

W

R

O

 M.

*𝒯*his week's

Ironing is not

done.

12

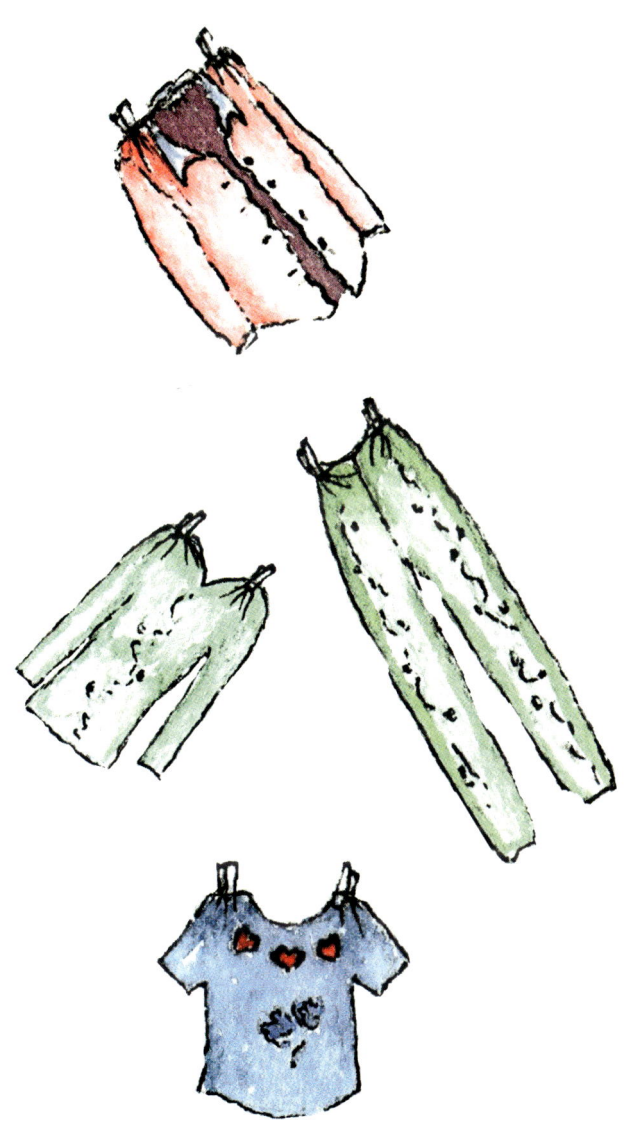

13

I don't want

to let you down,

but

I have a meeting.

It's

WAAAAAY

across town.

*M*y cell's been

riiiiiiiinging.

My boss is mad.

This is the

worst job

I've ever had.

*S*o,

*S*weet *H*annah,

please do forgive,

for I must work

so we both

can live.

But

you know those skates

you saw on line,

I'll buy you those

when I have

TIME.

As for

Mud Pies,

not today.

I'm sorry,

Hannah,

you'll have to wait."

So *H*annah

PLAYED

out in the sun.

*S*he wished her mom
would have some

FUN.

She wished for

mud pies

in the sand

and for her

mom to hold her hand,

but

*M*om was

tooooo

tired,

just

tooooo busy.

*J*ust what was

meant

by

"*in*

a

t I z z y"?

*M*ore days went by,

and

*H*annah

g r E **W**.

*S*he often wondered what to do.

She

surfed the net

and talked

with friends.

It seemed some days

would never end.

Before too long,

she was a teen.

A latchkey product, it did seem.

Her hair was *orange*,

some days *green*,

some days colors

in between.

She slept. She ate.

 She bought

more

bling.

Her choice of music was one

LOUD

SCREAM.

♪

S ome called it "**ROCK**."

Some called it " R A P ,"

but her momma simply

called it

"CRAP"!!!!!

♪   ♪

♪

$\mathcal{O}$ne day $\mathcal{H}$annah came

home from school. She was so

EXCITED

that she didn't know what to do.

She was going out on her very first

date. She would have to

HURRY.

She could hardly wait!

"Hey, Hannah, is that you? I got off early. I've been home since two. Grab Grandmother Young's old apron. Tie back your golden curls. Your hair does so remind me of mine as a little girl."

31

"*Gee*, Mom, I'm so

sorry, **but** I'm in such a

HURRY.

I'm going out on

my very first date.

I'll be home early.

Please don't

WORRY.

*M*om, I finally know

what it's like to be *sooo*,

sooo busy.

I guess as you would put it, Mom,

My life

is in

A TizZy.

My hair's a

mess.

My NAILS

aren't done,

so really, Mom,

I have to RUN.

*B*aking with you

would just be great,

But

I guess our little

Mud Pies

simply have to wait."

*M*om did think as she

stirred and scraped of those little

Mud Pies

she had made with

globs

of mud and a

touch of sand ...

that she had molded into a little

Chocolate Man.

*S*he also thought of all

those days that her precious

*H*annah

had begged to play…

of all those days

that she was

just

"*TOOOOO*

BUSY."

*W*hat a

PRICE

she had paid for

"IN A

TIZZY."

M ore days went by,
some short. ,

some **l o n g**.

*S*oon it was time for

*H*annah's senior prom.

An emerald dress

she did wear.

She placed Mom's old pearls

in her

golden hair.

Then Hannah **graduated**

and left her home,

leaving

Mud Pies

never done.

*S*he was now a

College Queen

with lots of

and

some study in between.

*S*he very seldom made

it home, **nor**

did she find

time

to pick up the phone.

*S*he finally met the

"**perfect man**."

An

elegant wedding

was now her plan,

a

Designer
Gown

with lots of lace,

an

illusion veil

around her face.

$\mathcal{M}$om was right there

by her side.

She looked at

$\mathcal{H}$annah

with such great pride-

her golden haired baby-

her

*W*here had all the years

flown in between?

$\mathcal{B}$efore too long,

$\mathcal{H}$annah was a mom.

She had a

golden haired

daughter

and a

handsome son.

She had a

full career

and a

suburban home,

but little time

to have much

FUN.

Her life was full,

Veeery busy,

just one more life of

"IN A TizZy."

*N*ever **TIME**

to stop to bake,

never **TIME** to

Mud Pies make.

N ever **TIME**

to visit Mom, for a brand

NEW CYCLE

had begun.

*T*he day soon came

*H*annah could

no longer wait.

*S*he had to keep this one

last date.

𝓕or in the night,

her mom had died.

*N*ow, *H*annah stood by her momma's side,

thinking of plans

they would always make…

of the little

Mud Pies

they had

never baked.

She thought of

times

she should have phoned,

of all the **times**

Mom was alone.

*H*er own golden curls were

NOW

silver streaked.

*T*iny WRINKLES

NOW

touched her cheeks.

as her
tears rushed
down
to
kiss
the earth,

*H*annah bent down

to take some

sand,

and when she

t o s s e d

it

from her hand,

it

    fell

        deep

into *her momma's*

GRAVE.

I_t

MIXED

with the dirt, and a

Mud Pie

made.

Quick order form
SEND THIS FORM

Fax orders: 662-449-0971.

Postal Orders:

Judy Hopkins

%Chocolate Gravy Books

1853 Ready Drive

Hernando, Mississippi 38632

Telephone 901-490-3669

Please send information on
_____other books
_____speaking engagements

Name:_____

Address:_____

City:_____

Telephone:_____

email address:_____

_____copies of Mud Pie @ $10.95
per copy. Plus $4.00 shipping, $2.00
each additional book.

_____Master Card

_____Visa

Card number:_____

Name on card:_____

Expiration date:_____

About the author

Judy Young, the youngest of five children, was born right in the middle of a cotton patch in Tyronza, Arkansas.

Her mother and the children chopped and picked cotton while her dad worked as a carpenter. This family literally owed their souls "to the company store." Consequently, all the children were motivated to seek a better life. They all set high goals, the main one being they did not want to pick cotton for the rest of their lives. All five of them went on to have very successful careers.

Judy graduated from Arkansas State University with a major in English. She lives with her husband, Robert Hopkins, in Hernando, Mississippi. She works as a real estate broker, a writer, and a speaker.

Presently, she is working on two other books *Seeds* and *Gifts*. Both of these books deal with children born in poverty who learn that true wealth comes from within.

For further information on upcoming books or to schedule Judy for a program, please call her at 901-490-3669 or e-mail her at judyhop@bellsouth.net.

About the illustrator

Emily Daniels Butler was also born in Tyronza, Arkansas; however, it was years later that she and Judy became friends. She is one of six children.

She was married to Donald Butler, who was a great inspiration to her before his death. She graduated from Arkansas State University and holds a Bachelor of Fine Arts degree. She is a free lance artist.